MONTHLY WEEKLY PLANNER 2015

Month of:

Sunday	Monday	Tuesday	Wednesday	Thursday	Friday	Saturday

Notes

Month of:

Sunday	Monday	Tuesday	Wednesday	Thursday	Friday	Saturday

Notes

Month of:

Sunday	Monday	Tuesday	Wednesday	Thursday	Friday	Saturday

Notes

Month of:

Sunday	Monday	Tuesday	Wednesday	Thursday	Friday	Saturday

Notes

Month of:

Sunday	Monday	Tuesday	Wednesday	Thursday	Friday	Saturday

Notes

Month of:

Sunday	Monday	Tuesday	Wednesday	Thursday	Friday	Saturday

Notes

Month of:

Sunday	Monday	Tuesday	Wednesday	Thursday	Friday	Saturday

Notes

Month of:

Sunday	Monday	Tuesday	Wednesday	Thursday	Friday	Saturday

Notes

Month of:

Sunday	Monday	Tuesday	Wednesday	Thursday	Friday	Saturday

Notes

Month of:

Sunday	Monday	Tuesday	Wednesday	Thursday	Friday	Saturday

Notes

Month of:

Sunday	Monday	Tuesday	Wednesday	Thursday	Friday	Saturday

Notes

Month of:

Sunday	Monday	Tuesday	Wednesday	Thursday	Friday	Saturday

Notes

Month of:

Sunday	Monday	Tuesday	Wednesday	Thursday	Friday	Saturday

Notes

Month of:

Sunday	Monday	Tuesday	Wednesday	Thursday	Friday	Saturday

Notes

Month of:

Sunday	Monday	Tuesday	Wednesday	Thursday	Friday	Saturday

Notes

Month of:

Sunday	Monday	Tuesday	Wednesday	Thursday	Friday	Saturday

Notes

Month of:

Sunday	Monday	Tuesday	Wednesday	Thursday	Friday	Saturday

Notes

Month of:

Sunday	Monday	Tuesday	Wednesday	Thursday	Friday	Saturday

Notes

Month of:

Sunday	Monday	Tuesday	Wednesday	Thursday	Friday	Saturday

Notes

Month of:

Sunday	Monday	Tuesday	Wednesday	Thursday	Friday	Saturday

Notes

Month of:

Sunday	Monday	Tuesday	Wednesday	Thursday	Friday	Saturday

Notes

Month of:

Sunday	Monday	Tuesday	Wednesday	Thursday	Friday	Saturday

Notes

Month of:

Sunday	Monday	Tuesday	Wednesday	Thursday	Friday	Saturday

Notes

Month of:

Sunday	Monday	Tuesday	Wednesday	Thursday	Friday	Saturday

Notes

Month of:

Sunday	Monday	Tuesday	Wednesday	Thursday	Friday	Saturday

Notes

Month of:

Sunday	Monday	Tuesday	Wednesday	Thursday	Friday	Saturday

Notes

Month of:

Sunday	Monday	Tuesday	Wednesday	Thursday	Friday	Saturday

Notes

Month of:

Sunday	Monday	Tuesday	Wednesday	Thursday	Friday	Saturday

Notes

Month of:

Sunday	Monday	Tuesday	Wednesday	Thursday	Friday	Saturday

Notes

Month of:

Sunday	Monday	Tuesday	Wednesday	Thursday	Friday	Saturday

Notes

Month of:

Sunday	Monday	Tuesday	Wednesday	Thursday	Friday	Saturday

Notes

Month of:

Sunday	Monday	Tuesday	Wednesday	Thursday	Friday	Saturday

Notes

Month of:

Sunday	Monday	Tuesday	Wednesday	Thursday	Friday	Saturday

Notes

Month of:

Sunday	Monday	Tuesday	Wednesday	Thursday	Friday	Saturday

Notes

Month of:

Sunday	Monday	Tuesday	Wednesday	Thursday	Friday	Saturday

Notes

Month of:

Sunday	Monday	Tuesday	Wednesday	Thursday	Friday	Saturday

Notes

Month of:

Sunday	Monday	Tuesday	Wednesday	Thursday	Friday	Saturday

Notes

Month of:

Sunday	Monday	Tuesday	Wednesday	Thursday	Friday	Saturday

Notes

Month of:

Sunday	Monday	Tuesday	Wednesday	Thursday	Friday	Saturday

Notes

Month of:

Sunday	Monday	Tuesday	Wednesday	Thursday	Friday	Saturday

Notes

Month of:

Sunday	Monday	Tuesday	Wednesday	Thursday	Friday	Saturday

Notes

Month of:

Sunday	Monday	Tuesday	Wednesday	Thursday	Friday	Saturday

Notes

Month of:

Sunday	Monday	Tuesday	Wednesday	Thursday	Friday	Saturday

Notes

Month of:

Sunday	Monday	Tuesday	Wednesday	Thursday	Friday	Saturday

Notes

Month of:

Sunday	Monday	Tuesday	Wednesday	Thursday	Friday	Saturday

Notes

Month of:

Sunday	Monday	Tuesday	Wednesday	Thursday	Friday	Saturday

Notes

Month of:

Sunday	Monday	Tuesday	Wednesday	Thursday	Friday	Saturday

Notes

Month of:

Sunday	Monday	Tuesday	Wednesday	Thursday	Friday	Saturday

Notes

www.ingramcontent.com/pod-product-compliance
Lightning Source LLC
LaVergne TN
LVHW082301150826
845677LV00009B/1684

* 9 7 9 8 8 6 9 4 5 5 2 0 8 *